To ...

Thank you for your
support!

Shine
Shondall Brewhite

Cover Design by: Kevin Vain, WEIN Design Agency

Interior Layout by: Rachel Knox, WEIN Design Agency

Cover Photographer: Kendra Kipkin

Social Media icons created by freepik - www.freepik.com

THE HOLY BIBLE, NEW INTERNATIONAL VERSION®, NIV® Copyright © 1973, 1978, 1984, 2011 by Biblica, Inc.™ Used by permission. All rights reserved worldwide.

ESV: STUDY BIBLE : ENGLISH STANDARD VERSION. Wheaton, Ill: Crossway Bibles, 2007. Used by permission. All rights reserved worldwide.

GOD'S WORD TRANSLATION. Cleveland, OH: Baker Publishing Group, 1995. Used by permission. All rights reserved worldwide.

HOLY BIBLE: NEW LIVING TRANSLATION. Wheaton, Ill: Tyndale House Publishers, 2004. Used by permission. All rights reserved worldwide.

ISBN: 978-0-578-88271-0

SHINE

Taking Back Control After Domestic Abuse

SHONDALE WILHITE

Contents

———◆———

Introduction

Your reality can change if you change your mind. I was ready to die to self and bury any and everything that would keep me from greatness. I had torn down the walls of brokenness, depression, and mediocrity so that I could be resurrected into the brand new me.

I survived what I believed to be the worst part of my life, and now I am ready to live my best life. I vowed to have no more sad days for the rest of my life. I thought to myself, it must be more to life than just going to work and paying bills. I had the mentality that I could not survive outside of a nine to five job, living paycheck to paycheck. I was so stuck and feeling so unfulfilled. I had so many dreams and aspirations that I never imagined coming true because I did not believe in myself.

I kept hearing that the best things in life are on the other side of fear, so I decided to take that leap of faith onto the other side. I had to make some life changing decisions, and I decided that it is my time to *S.H.I.N.E.*

Acknowledgments

-----◆-----

Giving honor to my Lord and Savior Jesus Christ, it is through Him that all things are possible.

To my mother and always my "Favorite Girl" who taught me to be independent. I honor you and give you accolades for being the best Mom you knew how to be to me. Thank you for surviving in your journey and handling matters the best you knew how. I give you your red roses now so that you can smell the fresh floral aroma that comes from the beautiful, blossomed bud that symbolizes love. I love you Mommy!

To my children (Alexis and D'Lane'), my reason for living and making a difference. I want you to know that I am working hard to fight off the giants this family has faced so that GiGi's babies (Ashton and Aliyah) and generations to come will not have to do so.

I love you Daddy Roy, Papa Ralph, and Mr. James these are the men in my life.

To Kenny and Yolanda founders of the Intentional Talk Radio Network, thank you for allowing me the platform to SHINE and talk about a subject matter dear to me, domestic and sexual abuse.

To Saundra Mosley, thank you for your partnership, your willingness to care for survivors of domestic violence and helping to make a difference in the world.

To all my family, friends and supporters thank you for believing in me and what I stand for and for all your continued support.

I love you,

Shondale

Luke 10:19

New Living Translation Bible

Look, I have given you authority over all the power of the enemy, and you can walk among snakes and scorpions and crush them. Nothing will injure you.

SPEAK OUT

chapter one

There is a time for everything.

Ecclesiastes 3:7 NIV
a time to tear and a time to mend, a time to be
silent and a time to speak,

*I*n **The Reality Behind The Illusion** we learned that silence is suffocating. No more keeping silent and pretending to be ok. What goes on in the house is no longer going to stay in the house. It is time to break the silence and speak out against all the toxicity in life. Some never get to this point and will take it all to their graves, but I chose to deal directly with my demons.

For years I could never break free of that stronghold of abuse, until one day, I got fed up! I was fed up with every toxic relationship I had ever encountered. It took me twenty years to do so, but as far as I am concerned, there is no statute of limitations on when an individual should unveil the darkness in their lives. Regardless of what the circumstance, it is their decision as to how they will handle it. Considering all the men that abused me, financial gain was certainly not the case, because they did not have any money. In my case, it was mainly to gain my freedom from it all so that I could finally heal and bury those giants. I did not care about who would not like how I went about my healing process or who it would affect. I did what was necessary for me. I pulled back the scab on wounds that were never fully healed and gained freedom unimaginable after doing so. I am breaking generational curses in my family and turning them into generational blessings. I am reaching out and helping other individuals that are suffering and crying out for help and making a difference. I am becoming the change I want to see. I speak out!

I am so glad that more and more people are coming forth to tell their truths about the abuse they have suffered. Both women and men are standing bold and unashamed to shine light on "that thing" that has traumatized their lives. #TimesUp for sexual harassment and the people in "power" that have continuously gotten away with inappropriate behavior in and out of the workplace. #TimesUp for the survivors of these crimes to feel like they must be silenced, because they would be blamed for the actions of someone else.

#MeToo is the outcry that so many people have spoken out. Is the world so conditioned to this kind of behavior that it has now become acceptable? Or is something REALLY going to be done about changing the consequences of it?

My desire is to create an environment where I can see myself for who I am, and not have to depend on "that thing" that took me out of my element; the job, the relationships, family and friends. Deal with the trauma and start healing, because when you own your circumstances than no one can use them against you.

So many things must happen for us to get to a breaking point, and finally say No More. I believe that life teaches us lessons and it will keep teaching us repeatedly until we get it. It is like we know better, but we still choose not to do better. No matter how bad life and people beat us down, we still sometimes accept that punishment, because we do not know our worth.

I affirm right now that I am worthy and that I deserve to be happy, healthy, and whole. No one else will have to defeat this giant of abuse for generations to come as I take it on with full force until it is dead. It is not the time to be silent, but a time to Speak Out!

HELP YOURSELF

chapter two

Psalms 40:13 God's Word Translation
[13] *O Lord, please rescue me! Come quickly to help me, O Lord!*

*I*t did not matter to me what other people's opinions were of me, because I was going to do what I wanted to do about my situation. At the time, my significant other did not have to isolate me from friends and family; I isolated myself. I did not care to hear about how stupid I was to be with someone that treated me so bad. But wait, I did not even know the difference of what it was like being treated good and bad. It was kind of like, if things were too good to be true, then I would expect something bad to happen for it to be normal. I was so confused about how I was supposed to feel about certain situations. When I was physically struck, I knew I felt pain and my feelings were hurt, but was that how I perceived love to be? After a few days, I missed him and wanted to see him and hear him say he was sorry; not I hate him, and I never want to see him again. Crazy, right? That went on for years, and I had to get to that point of wanting better for myself and my children, and only I could make that decision. No one else could make it for me.

I asked myself, "Is this the life you want to live?" And my answer was, Hell NO! My next question was, "So what are you going to do about it?" I came up with a plan. I realized in that moment that my response was going to determine the outcome of my circumstances.

I had to first remove myself from that environment of toxicity. I concluded that I cannot change people to be what I want them to be. It was hard enough trying to execute change in my own life. The one thing I knew was that I could not help myself by staying in "that thing" that was destroying all of me and everything of me.

Sometimes the hardest thing to do is to leave everything, but sometimes that is the best thing to do. What are you willing to sacrifice to take back your freedom and escape the slavery that has kept you bound for so long? Does fear have you so paralyzed that you cannot see past hopelessness, helplessness, and isolation? At some point I had to stop pretending and be truthful to myself. If I look like I have it altogether all the time, it is an indication to people that I do not need help. I tried not to look like what I was going through. It worked most of time. Coping mechanisms had become my best friend; smoking black and mild cigars, liquor and sex numbed me to all the pain I ever felt. That is why talking to someone is so important. If you continue to cry out silently, no one will hear you. Help Yourself! I had to change my mind to save my life.

I am out of the relationship, and in a safe place. Now what? What do I do when my abuser reaches out to me? If you share a phone plan, get rid of the phone, especially if it is not your wireless phone account. GPS tracking can be placed on the phone to track your whereabouts, or it may work to your advantage and track the abuser's whereabouts. Just to be safe; get rid of the phone. If you are able, get a prepaid phone or switch services altogether with a new phone number. When all else fails and you have your own phone plan, use your block features on your phone. It is one of my favorite phone features.

You may have to uproot from a job and even school but be willing to be temporarily inconvenienced to gain permanent peace of mind. Staying for the kids is another issue. That is not healthy either, because not only are you keeping yourself in danger, but now the kids are at risk. There is a lesson to be learned, and the kids are being taught by watching how everything around them is presented. Sons are taught that it is ok to abuse girls and control them. Daughters are taught it is ok to accept being abused and mistreated by boys and then another generation is impacted by domestic violence. Nothing is healthy about that situation. Help Yourself and your loved ones.

It is difficult to change your mind from the things you have been conditioned for so long. Train yourself to refrain from those thoughts. Do not sit back and wait for something tragic to happen before you decide to act, or worse, someone is planning your funeral.

Have a reason to live! Even if you do not have children or family. YOUR LIFE MATTERS! The enemy wants you to believe that your life does not matter and will use people to harm you or cause you to harm yourself. Resist feeling hopeless and know that there is a better life. Do not have a "what's the use" mindset just because someone else has devalued you. When you see money on the ground that has been walked over and overlooked, it still holds its value. It will eventually be picked up and used for its purpose.

It is important to learn how to love yourself. If you do not love you or nothing about you, then how can you expect anyone else to love you any more than you do? People will treat you as good as you treat yourself. Removing myself from the chaos helped me to be able to get to know me. I learned some things about me and what I like. I like movies, amusement parks, ice cream, traveling, dancing, journaling, and my peace of mind. I started doing those kinds of things with my kids. Then I found myself smiling and feeling happy. It was a good feeling. I looked at everything that was around me and suddenly realized that I was blessed. I had my beautiful healthy babies, a roof over my head, food, a car, my health, a job, and a reason to live. But when I looked in the mirror, I did not like what I saw. The outer me nor the inner me. Years ago, I heard someone tell a good friend of mine that I looked like a "dope fiend" trying to dress up when we were at my daughter's 2nd birthday party. I remembered that comment and my good friend laughed. It was very hurtful. I was already a bit self-conscious about my weight, but I did not say anything. I started to eat things that would make me gain weight; then I was too fat for the people. Thankfully, I stopped living for people and started just "doing me". I had come to the realization that I am more than the names that people call me. I always dressed nice and I would do different things with my hair and makeup; that took care of the outer me. But I was still struggling with the inner me. What about my soul? There was a lot of that toxic residue left over from all my unhealthy relationships. My soul felt empty. It was dark, hardened and closed off. I needed a savior, so I went to the Word of God. That is when it started getting personal:

Psalm 23:1 New International Version (NIV)
¹ The Lord is MY shepherd, I lack nothing.

I had to figure out how to detox my mind from all the negativity that clogged it for so long. The first thing I did was search for motivational speakers, sermons, quotes, videos, or songs to pour into my soul. I did that for months and I still practice it daily. It is amazing how something as simple as what you listen to all day will impact your life! Then I changed the association of people in my circle. Since I was "growing" in a different direction, my desire was to be in affiliation with people that were already where I wanted to be. Growth and development are essential for success. Learning new behavioral patterns and skill sets gave me the confidence I needed to feel empowered. I actually helped myself!

IGNITE YOUR FIRE

chapter three

Speak life into yourself!

> *Proverbs 18:21 (GW)*
> *The tongue has the power of life and death, and those who love to talk will have to eat their own words.*

This is the process that would make me nervous. I remember being very much dependent on Section 8 housing (government assistance). It was help for low income individuals to be able to afford decent housing. At one particular time, I lived in a three-bedroom house, and I believe I was laid off from my job. I had an appointment to renew my housing, and because I was getting unemployment benefits, it was considered income. My rent went from $740 to $719 a month. I decided to decline the assistance, because I did not want to deal with all the politics for a twenty-one-dollar difference. I had been on an escrow program within Dallas Housing Authority. It was like a savings account. The program would match the amount of rent I paid each month for five years; given it was paid on time. After my five years, I had $20k in my escrow account, and I requested my money. The ideal goal was to purchase a home, but I chose to use some of the money to send my son to college. The people that I shared that info thought I was crazy to decline the assistance with no job. I was basically putting limitations on myself by staying on the program, as well as being labeled as a "low income" individual. I did not want that label anymore. I want the label of prosperity! It was very scary being self- sufficient after having that help for so long, but here I am years later still making a way on my own. I proved to myself that I can do this thing called life. Thank God for His grace and mercy!

I had settled into a two- bedroom apartment unit once I removed myself from housing assistance. I was not very satisfied with it, but it was one of those "it'll do for now" places. I did not want to relocate from that area, because my son was about to be a senior in high school. Once he graduated, I was preparing to get him off to college (Prairie View A&M University). I was so proud of him! He had been accepted into the marching band on the drum line. I told him that it was my time to live my life, the adult life. I downsized and moved near downtown Dallas. I had done my part of getting him and his sister through school and providing them with what they needed along the way. I do not know who was more excited; me moving into my new place or him getting off to college.

That "it will do for now" mentality was gone. I upgraded myself to have all the nice things I desired in my space. It felt good to be doing things on my own. I was taking control of my life.

Psalm 37:4 ESV
Delight yourself in the Lord, and he will give
you the desires of your heart.

I love to travel, and I wanted to travel more. I remember when I worked for an ethnic hair care company that sent me on lots of business trips. They would always be fun trips. We had customers from all over the world, and I got the opportunity to meet a lot of our international customers in person in Las Vegas for the annual Cosmoprof Exhibition. I went to LA, New Orleans (Essence Festival), and the Gospel Explosion in Georgia for product promotions just to name a few. I really liked that job. It allowed me to experience a different side of the hair care industry. I worked in supply chain and logistics. I was learning so much and feeling pretty amazing.

I was a licensed cosmetologist when I graduated high school and had worked in a salon for a little while. I had to move into the corporate arena, because I had a family and needed the benefits.

I worked in numerous fields and picked up quite a few skills as well just from temporary assignments at various companies. Although I did not earn a lot of money, I was able to take care of myself and my children; despite what others thought. I had to sometimes keep negative people out of my ear that thought they could do a better job than me when it came to my children.

Over the years, I have also taken advantage of opportunities to develop my mind and skill set by completing continuing education courses, business administration classes, leadership training (Toastmasters International), personal development and business training to generate multiple streams of income. Growth and development should be a daily practice. You never get too old or wise to learn more.

As I reflect, I was already doing everything pretty much on my own, so how did I ever feel like I could not make it on my own? Oh right, I was manipulated into thinking that I could not, and I believed it. You live and learn. It took me awhile to figure it all out, so I had to endure multiple toxic relationships. After the physical abuse with one, it was emotional and verbal abuse with the others.

When I changed my mind from accepting anything that life threw at me, I was able to forgive myself for making the same mistakes repeatedly. I sometimes think about all the times I allowed myself to get into situations that I could have avoided. Then wondered why I did "that thing" I would regret later. Whether I believed it or not, I had choices. Everything is a choice. I choose the clothes I wear, the food I eat, the jobs I worked, my hairstyles, and I even chose my significant others. So now when I choose things that do not work for me, I change my mind and choose something else.

Change can be good! I often thought that if things had to change that it would force me to get out of my comfort zone. I had to be comfortable with being uncomfortable if I wanted to be successful.

NEVER LOOK BACK

chapter four

Isaiah 43:18-19 NLT
But forget all that— it is nothing compared to
what I am going to do. For I am about to do
something new. See, I have already begun! Do
you not see it? I will make a pathway through
the wilderness. I will create rivers in the dry
wasteland.

I have come too far to turn back now! I am stronger because I finally know my worth. I pushed through suffocating in silence and now I SPEAK OUT. I took a good look in the mirror and saw that I was dying and decided to HELP MYSELF. Then I started to shake things up a bit to IGNITE MY FIRE and now I will NEVER LOOK BACK!

Shondale, allow me to introduce to you ShonShine. ShonShine is my alter ego's name. She is a brand-new woman that has transformed from brokenness and hopelessness to bold and unashamed. It must have been something that my mother saw awaken in me, because she started addressing me as ShonShine. I took ownership of it and ran with it. I like that I have control over my life and not feel intimidated by anyone anymore. I can now express myself in ways unapologetically. I can defend myself and stand firm on what I believe. When I discover that I have drifted too far away from my life- line (God's Word), I know how to pull myself back to shore.

For instance, every person that I have dated has tried to come back into my life after the breakup. Somehow, I found myself on the phone with an ex-fiancé. After a couple of days of talking, I realized that I was about to get bamboozled! I had this conversation with myself. I said, "Self, what the hell are you doing?" I started thinking about all that had transpired for him to become an "ex" and I quickly used my favorite feature on my phone…BLOCK! Always remember why you left a toxic relationship; it will quickly get you back on track!

I cannot afford to have people coming into my life that do not have my best interest. If I sense any discernment at all, that is my queue to refrain from whatever it is. ShonShine holds Shondale accountable for her actions, because Shondale is still healing every day. ShonShine is bold and courageous and protects herself from anything or anybody that comes against her. She has gained strength through all her battles. She is confident. She has a way of connecting with people through sharing her truths, and she needs no validation from anyone when it comes to her worth. Other people's opinion of her is irrelevant. The old Shondale is gone and ShonShine was resurrected. There had to be an accountability partner for her, even if it had to be created in her mind. ShonShine sets boundaries that no one can cross and stands guard to fight off the things of the past.

S. H. I. N. E.

EVOLVE

chapter five

I gave myself permission to pursue my dreams!
I had to finally put my faith to work.

James 2:17 New International Version (NIV)
[17] In the same way, faith by itself, if it is not ac-
companied by action, is dead.

I had to put an expiration date on my complaining. I was complaining about everything; my stagnant life, the people around me, my job, and the people on the job. This was too much. I cried daily because I did not want to be there anymore. Then the question was posed, why don't you just apply for another position? It was deeper than having another position. It was about building my own empire and creating a legacy that will be passed down from generation to generation. I am a servant, and my purpose is to serve people that have suffered through toxic relationships and help them to transform from brokenness to wholeness.

I read an article that said, "You can control your mind by what you feed it, and that becomes your mindset, but your mindset is what controls you." My mind has been changed to transform my life.

Romans 12:2 NLT
Do not copy the behavior and customs of this world, but let God transform you into a new person by changing the way you think. Then you will learn to know God's will for you, which is good and pleasing and perfect.

After fighting, kicking, and screaming, I stopped complaining and acted. I made up in my mind that I was going to reinvent myself and leave corporate America. It was one of the scariest things I have ever done, but I knew that faith and fear could not reside together. "Fear is just false evidence appearing real," as Lisa Nichols says. I tried to schedule an appointment to get my head examined, because I thought I had lost my mind! My family and friends even thought I was crazy. I was so stressed, and I soon realized it was location frustration. It had everything to do with where I was in my life. The day I put in my resignation, I was given a pay increase and I left the money on the table. It was just time to move on.

I figured I would leave on my own terms as opposed to being involuntarily released. My complaining ended October 8, 2018.

I took a leap of faith with no backup plan. I was feeling perplexed about what I would do for money when I left my job. After talking to a young lady, I met at an event with a similar story, I became an independent contractor for rideshare (Uber & Lyft). It was so ironic because we had only talked a couple of times. It was a good feeling to manage my own schedule with all the flexibility I needed. I had not been my own boss since my early 20s when I was a licensed hairstylist. I have no regrets.

My plan is to continue my advocacy for domestic and sexual abuse and tour the world. I guess I had to start in the trenches, riding around town. I have reached thousands in private conversations through sharing my story. I believe that my authenticity is what resonates with people.

My first book The Reality Behind the Illusion was a three- time nominee; the Christian Literary Award 2018 and (2) Indie Author Legacy Awards 2019. It has awarded me so many opportunities for book signings, radio and TV appearances, author expos, and speaking engagements.

That was only the beginning! The evolution continues and I am excited about the journey ahead. My bio is continuously growing, and I am so glad I took the risk to follow my dreams. There is still so much more to come. I have a lot of struggles, but according to the Word of God it is to be expected.

John 16:33 NLT
I have told you all this so that you may have peace in me. Here on earth you will have many trials and sorrows. But take heart because I have overcome the world.

I realized that there was a shift happening in my life, because a lot of the things that I used to do, I just do not desire to do anymore. When I received my first paid keynote speaking opportunity, it was in October 2018 (Domestic Violence Awareness Month). That meant so much to me because of the passion I have to end domestic violence. In the same month of that year, I also had the opportunity to travel abroad on my dream vacation to Dubai. It was so amazing! It was definitely a dream come true!

I am enjoying life and doing things that make me happy all while being single. I always thought that the only way I could be happy was to have someone else in my life to make me happy and whole. I was so misguided and lost. I used to think it was attractive for someone to have control over me; until I felt all the side effects. Now I have complete control over my own life. That means not having anyone tell me what, when and how I should do things or with whom.

I have yet to reach my highest peak of excellence, but I have come into wholeness. I am comfortable with all of me; flaws and all, but consistently improving.

I am still working on my mental state of mind, and that is a daily work in progress. I thank God for my new life. I like it so much better now than it was before. This may not seem to be much of an accomplishment to some, but it sure has made me a better person. I have my health and strength, a beautiful family, and friends, I have the things that I need and some of my wants and I am alright with that.

The best is yet to come as I continue to EVOLVE, and I will not dare allow anyone to dim my light, because it is my time to S.H.I.N.E.

This is just a peek at some opportunities that have come to me, because I decided that I deserve better.

Co-Author the #1 best seller We Are Survivors Visual

Empowerment Journal of inspirational quotes that is live in five countries (Africa, Spain, Italy, France, and UK).

Co-Author Home Anthology an Antidote of Creative Expression by Michael Guinn

Actress in the domestic violence stage play (Scarred for Life) David Moore Production

Host of my own radio talk show, SHINE with Shondale on the Intentional Talk Radio Network. Now playing on Pandora, Spotify, Stitcher, IHeart and more to come.

Formed a support group with a partner on Facebook for women, Healing Support After Domestic Violence and hosted our 1st annual We Have a Voice Domestic Violence Awareness Summit in October 2020.

Mentor women impacted by DV all over the world.

Member of the African American Domestic Violence Council headed by The Family Place.

A speaker at The Best You Virtual Expo LA

My first book The Reality Behind the Illusion is still finding its way into places that my body has not reached YET!

Live Your Life!

Epilogue: The Legacy

God's revelation says that, "I am Alpha and Omega, the first and last the last, the beginning and the end."

Even though the world is constantly changing; God's word is constant and never changes.

If you just believe that all things are possible; put your faith and trust in God and become unstoppable.

Who cares about your circumstances; because we serve a loving God that gives us second chances?

A chance to redeem ourselves and repent of sins; then die to self and be resurrected again.

Change our mind and change our heart; from God's love we should never depart.

Encourage yourself regardless of what nay sayers

say and slay every giant that gets in your way.

Learn all you can develop and grow; so that when the enemy tries to test you, you will that you know…

One day, when the glory comes it will be ours, oh it will be ours (John Legend)

Philippians 4:13 says I can do all things; so, do not let anyone discourage you from your hopes and your dreams.

Leave a legacy by changing the game so that your great grandkids kids will know your name.

When you look in the mirror and you do not like what you see; then change the image to what you want it to be.

Because if you do not love you or nothing about you; then how can you expect anyone else to love you more than you do?

A change is going to come when God's will be done.

So free yourself of generational curses and feeling suppressed; and be the first but not the last to be generationally blessed.

In Loving Memory of the Life and Legacy of Granddaddy

Mr. Walter "Buck" Moore

Our Hero

11/10/1913- 3/09/2019

And my beautiful Grandparents

Olentha Wilhite (Big Daddy) and Marie Wilhite (Big Mama) R.I.H

Shondale Wilhite

AUTHOR | SPEAKER | RADIO TALK SHOW HOST

Shondale is a native of Dallas, TX. She is a domestic violence and sexual abuse advocate. Her advocacy is very dear to her because she is a survivor and determined to make a difference in the lives of others.

Shondale has been featured in Voyage Dallas Magazine, Author Expos in NY and Dallas, appeared on Everyone Has a Story on CANTV (Chicago), several other TV and radio interviews and over forty news outlets.

Shondale's first book the Reality Behind the Illusion can be purchased on amazon domestically and internationally.

Shondale is also a member of the African American Domestic Violence Council and has worked for fortune 500 companies. One of the greatest gifts she has ever given herself was the gift of FREEDOM!

For booking or speaking opportunities contact Author Shondale Wilhite at:

 shondalewilhite@gmail.com

Shine With Shondale
Pandora Radio
Intentional Talk Radio Network

Shondale Wilhite
The Reality Behind the Illusion:
Defeating Giants of Sexual and
Domestic Abuse

 @ Shondale Wilhite

 @ Shondale Wilhite

 @ Shondale Wilhite

Made in the USA
Columbia, SC
25 June 2021

40642500R00028